NEWS OF THE WORLD

Peter Fallon

NEWS
OF THE
WORLD

Selected and New Poems

for Skip and Lyn
at their home
in Lakeville,
with great affections
and thanks, too —
— Peter
October 1998

Gallery Books

News of the World: Selected and New Poems
is first published
simultaneously in paperback
and in a clothbound edition
on 23 April 1998.

The Gallery Press
Loughcrew
Oldcastle
County Meath
Ireland

ISBN 1 85235 214 0 (*paperback*)
        1 85235 215 9 (*clothbound*)

The Gallery Press acknowledges the financial assistance
of An Chomhairle Ealaíon / The Arts Council, Ireland,
and the Arts Council of Northern Ireland.

Contents

for Jean,
Adam and Alice

PART ONE

Selected Poems:
News of the World

Long live the weeds ...
— Gerard Manley Hopkins, 'Inversnaid'

A Woman of the Fields

She stands in the middle of a field
and says she'll stand there
for years.

— But come the summer
and the mower's path?
She'll be grass.

— Come Autumn
and the chainsaw's teeth?
She'll be wood.

— And Winter?
She'll be fodder, fruit of fields.
Spring she'll grow again.

She'll grow again I know.
An other woman
shades my meadow

and I mind this:
a blade of her hair in a book
and her big kiss.

The Lost Field

for Tanya and Wendell Berry

Somewhere near Kells in County Meath
a field is lost, neglected, let by common law.

When the Horse Tobin went to the bad
and sold a farm and drank the money
there was outlying land we couldn't find.

The maps weren't marked.
My people farmed the farm.
They looked and asked about.
They kept an ear to the ground.

They asked the Horse himself.
He handed out handfuls of fivers,
cups of whiskey, and sang dumb.

His sister said, he's fearless but no fool.
He has a fame for fighting
and carried far from himself
caused cases for the County Nurse.
I can't help you. I pray to God
he'll come back to his senses.

Then I came home from Dublin
to take my place.
My part in this is reverence.

Think of all that lasts. Think of land.
The things you could do with a field.
Plough, pasture, or re-claim. The stones
you'd pick, the house you'd build.

Don't mind the kind of land,
a mess of nettles even,
for only good land will grow nettles.
I knew a man shy from a farm
who couldn't find a weed
to tie the pony to.

Imagine the world
the place your own windfalls could fall.

I'm out to find that field, to make it mine.

Spring Song

It was as if
someone only had to say
Abracadabra
to set alight
the chestnut
candelabra.

Bloom and blossom
everywhere, on furze,
on Queen Anne's Lace.
A breeze blew
cherry snows
on the common place.

Weeds on walls;
the long grass
of the long acre;
the elderberry bushes
blazing thanks
to their maker.

Loud leaves of
southside trees,
the reticent buds of ash,
the reach of undergrowth
were voices, voices,
woods' panache.

Cub foxes.
Cock pheasants braced
themselves to sing.
The white thorn flowers
were the light infantry
of Spring

marching down the headlands.
A new flock flowed
through a breach,
a makeshift gate.
And this is heaven:
sunrise through a copper beech.

The Old Masters

First there was the wonder of their work.
We read their lines and outlines, took asunder
tops of walls, roof remains. Roofing.
A nailbar underneath a granite hundredweight –
how they got up what we could not get down we wonder

yet. We put our plans away. We rode and tied
the horse of their instruction, used all we could
again. We unclenched fists of ivy, hammered home
spiked stays. Wallplates, rafters, runners –
timber felled and treated from a Loughcrew wood.

We nailed sheet iron, shelter for the hay,
the settled flock. That shed's founded on rock
and finished for our time like the work
of woodsmen who, when they have finished
chopping, chop the chopping-block.

Windfalls

He is foddering cattle at a gap,
the windiest part of the field.
They were giving out a gale last night,
strong westerlies and warnings.
'That's the wind that peeled

potatoes in New York!'
It skimmed the top of the Atlantic
and tipped it over Ireland.
The blue twine of a bale
is slicing perished fingers. Some antic

power flipped a roof into an outfield;
an undressed outhouse shivers by its edge.
The dervish dance of sleet and hail
has crusted backs of sheep,
cruel comfort by a whitethorn hedge.

Wild days and wicked weather
cut to the bone — not a lot to set store
by. They're troubled times.
'True. They're troubled times.
There's men dying now never died before.'

He has seen it all and lived to tell.
A cloudbreak lightens his eyes' frown.
'Don't fear or fret. They made the back
to bear the burden.' He'll saw and split
the windfalls when the wind dies down.

from *Eye to Eye*

Grain on the roadside,
small change of a fortune;

his geese are gone from goslings.

❧

He has pitched his fill.
He is leaning against the tailboard
of a low trailer:

'The man who couldn't save hay
the year
needs help with more than the baler.'

❧

He worked with
and not against the weather.
A happy man.
Trade is good and the grass
is gone. The last time we were together

at a harvest dance,
his silhouette in
a lather of sweat
marvelled at the size of the crowd.
You'd need a haircut to get in.

The full of the hall and more
in the yard. When he'd shaken
and held my partner's hand
he turned to enquire,
'Is this the wife, or grass you've taken?'

He'd grow grass
on a stone.
He has humoured a farm
into fruitfulness.

His little ado,
his give and take,
leave the hay to make
and the lambs to do.

He stares at it, eye to eye,
the storm;
the man who cuts winter wood's
twice warm.

The whitethorn's as green
as the black —
he has broadcast seed
from an old sack-

apron and is taking
his ease.
Not in thunder or lightning,
he sees the bounty of God in a breeze.

Carnaross 2

She was teeming the potatoes
in the scullery when his brother
stood himself on the step
and asked to use the 'phone.

We overheard, as was the way,
quiet talk. Then she said
I'm sorry for your trouble
and told him to sit down.
She said she'd wet the tea.

First it was a withered calf.
Then this and that. One thing
led to another. Soon
he wouldn't bother his head
to read *The Celt*.
The bad word on the wind
weighed heavily on him.

And maybe he touched the little girls,
and maybe he didn't.

But he went to the bog wood.
The rope was found missing
when his brother went to milk.

I was told don't be gawking
and sent to the woodshed for sticks.
When the yard gate shut
I heard her say
there was always an if about him,
him and all his others.

The Rag-tree, Boherard

They might have come on the wind,
these rags and tatters, or drifted down
the current of the ditch to dangle there
like seaweed. They were the bright hand-me-down

foliage of that thorn tree in winter.
Poor sinners came, warts and all,
for the holy water of that holy well.
They left loose tokens of a patchwork shawl,

prayed, and promised to return.
They say it stood since God was a boy,
a twisted stick of offerings
no weather could destroy.

It fell in our time. This was told to me
by one of a lost community
at the crossroads of Knocklough,
that lived from hand to mouth, past pity,

and held the rest of the world
long in the gaze of its one eye.
It will pass like their names,
Snows, Laws, into the legends of incubi.

Well they might have hung their coat
on that hawthorn bush at Boherard
or come to kneel near the church
where, late one night, at the graveyard

gate, a big tree moved. We heard it stood
three hundred years, heard tell of the way
it simply took up roots and walked.
Anyway it moved. Or so they say.

The Meadow

We have welded the towbar
and turned the mower's eighteen blades –
the mower, the meadow reiver.
We'll work all night, by the last
and first light and, in between, by the minutes
of moonlight. This is hay fever.

For weeks we've watched smudged fields
weighed down by mean July.
We've heard them broadcast
brightness and woken to wet weather.
We'd be better off watching Billy McNamee
than paying heed to the radio forecast.

When meadows grow he finds a way.
We say we'll trust our own translation
of the sky and start to mow
this evening. We'll be racing the rain.
Tomorrow we'll turn and turn again.
Midweek we'll set the bob to row.

Then we'll bale. We did that then,
headed the stacks with loose hay
from the headlands. We thought we'd won
until we heard of loss that rotted in rows
and stopped aftergrass. Insult to injury.
Talk everywhere of fusty fodder, self-combustion.

Ten years ago we built ten thousand bales,
two of us, and climbed the mountain
afterwards to rest in forestry that mearns
sheep pasture, a famine field
of lazy beds. We gazed down from
a cemetery of thirty cairns

across a stonewalled country.
Stacks of bales in circles – our work
stood out like harvest monoliths.
A thousand stones, standing,
speaking, leaning, lying stones,
the key- and cornerstones of myths . . .

Our farms began in those.
It was as if we tried to read the signs
of Newgrange from the moon. A thistle splinter
brought us back to earth
knowing that we'd gathered of its plenty
enough to fortify our care against the winter.

The Late Country

Come again and we'll go back
to the late country. On the long way in
we'll hone an appetite
for drinks and stories. A knock. A silent
password. A 'Come in'. We're home and dry.
We'll see things there in a different light.

They'll be waiting, three wise men,
giving and taking all the news.
'Were there many at the mart?'
'There were often more
at the ringing of a pig.'
'Your man bought calves? Did he part

with much?' 'He did. He paid
two prices for them.' 'Well tell me this,
does the same man have a clue
about stock, or does he only know
about everything?' 'He's no daw.'
'He's not.' 'That's a fact and true.'

'His father was a great judge
of a live lamb.' 'He was.' 'But the other one's
all hot air and graces . . . '
'The brother? Stop. He wouldn't know
to come in from the rain.' 'I suppose . . . '
'You may be sure.' 'He wouldn't be at the races.'

They'll order the same again,
their backs to a neighbour
who is falling asleep and off his stool.
He has been stood up.
He is heard to mumble,
'Am I an eejit or a fool?'

He has lost his head in a cloud
of smoke from a cigarette and says
to himself, 'She might have sent word . . . '
He hears his uncle's echo,
'Aye. And a pig might fly.
But it's not a likely bird.'

He is drinking to forget.
He has yet to learn that bad beats worse.
Remember when we lingered in the dark
the night before the day Joe Tynan
bumped into a dog and pleaded,
'Bite me but don't bark.'

And someone said we'll have one
for the road – and one for the ditch –
when that knock came
and the law came in. They started
asking things they knew already,
'Name?'

and noted men muttering in Irish
and forgetting their addresses,
observed the clumsy pantomime
of men with drink taken standing
straight upright, blinded by the light.
'Have you any idea of the time?'

'I suppose it's late.'
And the guard we knew loomed
in battle dress beside us like the Prince
of Darkness. 'I'm surprised at you.
I thought you knew better . . . ' '*You're*
surprised? Sure I thought I left ages since.'

Country Music

He is stuck in the mud of four weeks' rain
backing a tractor through a gap
to fodder beasts. They worship at an altar
of a trailer with the tailboard off,

up to their knees in a muck moraine.
They swish the thuribles of their tails, slap
incense breath on the silage psalter,
grain, torn cud; a smothered cough.

He is stuck in the mud of that profane
ritual, his hundred fathers' handicap
of squids and squalls, and asks for a hand. We falter
and spring free. Now I'm dragging water to a frozen trough,

one with them, their muttered Bollocks, Shits and Fuck its,
a cursèd yoke beneath a pair of splashing buckets.

Possessed

They have made halves of themselves
to manage and have chosen a spot
without a thought
to dangle on the nub of one same branch
twines of bales by the knot

where they tend winter stock,
a cow that calved. They've dragged hay
and water down a right
of way. Cat's cradles wave in the wind.
They'll have made by March a May-

pole — if they live that long.

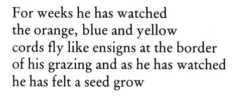

For weeks he has watched
the orange, blue and yellow
cords fly like ensigns at the border
of his grazing and as he has watched
he has felt a seed grow

in the mind. For every word
in his house was a nudge
of neighbours' trespass and transgression,
of wrongs done and disputes, and every look
was fuel on the fire of a grudge.

It wasn't off the ground he licked it.

No, that row started on the Ark. But was he
ever all right in the head? He was erratic,
but if you owed him money
he'd be right enough. He didn't know
the end of strength. Remember he'd be acrobatic

in a pub or public place — handstands,
cartwheels for a pound. A rush of blood
was little wonder
the way that he was pushed. And he began to plan
the end of them whose family name was mud

the morning something snapped.

For the broody mind must hatch.
And so he planted in a ditch
himself and all he needed — lock,
stock, and barrel, and a cartridge belt.
'I'll scratch that itch,'

he might have said
before he brought to its knees
a family and an ordinary afternoon.
One shot and another. A calf bawled at a gap.
The birds that scattered from the trees

flew in all directions.

We heard and had to wonder. What was it
came over him? What possessed him
on a given day and not
a million miles from here
to do the like? A whim.

He'd cattle of his own to fodder,
which he did. Then he remembered to give
up himself. 'There's been an incident.
I'll likely need solicitors. You know yourself.
One of those things you have to live

with — if you're let or able.'

Airs and Graces

Nine times out of ten
he'd be complaining
and the tenth
condemning neighbours' stock
or the way they kept their fences.
Or he'd be crowing about
something of his own.
Cock of the walk,
a cut above buttermilk –
his geese were swans apparently.
The harvest moon perched
in his *Pendula* pear tree.

He went astray one winter.
They started soon to say
he's not the full shilling.
And someone said he'd take
so much in his stride
he hadn't feet on the ground
at all. A head in the clouds,
from which advantage he could see
no more nor the next man,
a world throughother.
When pressed he'd say
if it's not one thing, it's another.

The night he struck
the woman of the house
and shut her in the meal shed
they had it from the daughters.
He'd taken them to bed
once and again
and one conceived.

The doctor came and called the guards.
A cousin came to help
start the milking-machine
and stayed to finish foddering. There was
no moon. The stars were few and far between.

Fallow

To hear the old men speak
of the Bluebell Wood or Ferny Field
is to chance on something holy,
but I thought these were only names,
Deerfield, Deerpark, Buckminster,
until we came upon them.

I'd seen outliers from hunts
but here in a medium of meadow
they moved in concert as much at home
as otters in water, hawks in the air,
a well-known secret, adrift unminded,
past paddock and three gates.

Far from the breacher beasts around
they'd pause at an opening for hours
before entering to eat,
and these never left this park
in a handful of families' times.
Once they were rendered tame by frequent

visitations, then wary of hounds, snares,
poachers' lights, and the keeper's beat
fallen short of their runways, broken ground,
and innocent of crooked will,
like a field untilled,
knew only to seed among themselves.

Someday in winter I'll watch
the old collapse at their loving
and a new buck continue a cycle
begun with the shedding of velvet
as light as their courage
or the step of their young.

from *Gravities*

A ewe moves northward
to a gate, her lambs in tow.
Another follows and again
the night's migration

is begun. Thin lines of sheep
approach a slope, the frantic calls
resume, the mothers' for lambs,
the lambs' for milk.

And I've known men
tell weather by this moment.

❧

She kept a compact since tup-time,
the cross-bred hogget in the shed.
She sprang proud teats
and grew a bellows in the belly
to heave and shove against defeat.

I reached to help. My seeing fingers
turned a couple in the womb.
I pulled by front feet, held by hind
until they breathed. Cords and cleanings
dangled; the lambs, the lambs stood up.

Caesarean

They were clouds come down to ground to yean,
clouds from which clouds of breathing broke.
We went out, night and day, again and again,
to check or correct. One was clearheaded.
She hadn't the fire to make that kind of smoke.

She stood humpbacked, worn out.
We knew she could no longer carry.
One slim chance. No time to doubt
that we would learn what to do by doing.
We did not hesitate or hurry.

This would take its own time. We lay
her down and gently pulled wool from her sides.
We were clearing the way.
We went for towels, soap, beestings, and the gun.
Her lambs could swim in the rough tides

of her death. We shot her to save some drib
from loss, save her pain. She opened like a bloom
beneath the red script of the scalpel's nib
and we found twins, abandoned, perfectly
formed in the warm nest of her womb.

Premature. Too young to live. We had thought
of everything but this, what could not be guessed.
That she was ready and they were not.
They lay like kindlings dazed by daylight,
the tips of their tongues, their front feet pressed

to dive as one into the waters
of the world. We knelt close to hear a heart,
heard our own and thought it one of theirs. Daughters
of death, they'd never know their gifts,
the everyday miracles of which they were part.

They were part instead of that sacrifice
of the whole. James shrugged a smile.
The lambs pulsed once or twice,
and died. We had done what we could. Now there
were other things to do. We said nothing for a while.

Neighbours

If your sheep strayed they mightn't be returned.
His? They'd be collected
and maybe more along with them.

He was known to all and nodded to
in company when others talked,
he whose flock grew overnight
and not by buying or breeding,
whose brands were smudged, and who sheared early.

I've heard men say, 'He'd take the eye
of your head.' Aye, and the milk from your tea.

Fostering

He was lost in the blizzard of himself
and lay, a cold white thing, in a drift
of afterbirth. Another stood to drink dry spins.
I put him with the foster ewe who sniffed

and butted him from his birthright, her milk.
I took the stillborn lamb and cleft
with axe on chopping-block its head,
four legs, and worked the skin apart with deft

skill and rough strength. I dressed the living lamb
in it. It stumbled with the weight, all pluck,
towards the ewe who sniffed and smelled and licked
raiment she recognized. Then she gave suck —

and he was Esau's brother and I Isaac's wife
working kind betrayals in a field blessed for life.

Dipping Day

An Indian raindance is nothing on this,
not with our *Hai, hup, hey, hoo,*
and Jimmy dancing with a stick.
They'll go where you don't want
and won't where you do.

He's shouting 'Right. Right, she said,'
and saying they'll follow if one goes.
But now they're steadfast.
Twice a year and they remember –
last year's lambs, rams, ewes –

remember the passage, the plank they walk,
the ritual where we baptize
all the flock for ticks, flies. This
is the high jump backwards. They are hung
on the rope of their surprise.

We have our stations, Jimmy, John, and I.
We grab them by the front
and pull them back. They sink and swim.
James dunks them again. There is
the annual refrain: you push and I'll grunt.

Dipping day. They stand in a pen, dripping.
We take a rest. There's talk, an anecdote
about the day the boss fell in.
Right, I ask, ready? and hear for the hundredth
time, 'Right, she said. But she never wrote!'

The Herd

I studied in the hedge school
and learned religions are a cod.
They're all the one.
Ask any fool.
Every lamb's a lamb of God.

Catholics

The man at the bar is cursing women;
he hates his wife and loves his mother
and tells who'll hear of the whores
he's ridden. When they hadn't a woman
they improvised, himself and another.

Behind the ballrooms of their need
they actualised their monstrous art,
and in the dark they dreamt of Mary.
And maybe I'm as bad —
I've come for the loan of an ass and cart

and listen to deeds at the Parish Sports
that gorged a greed that knew no bounds.
'Sport is right! That woman's a mother
in England now.' And he escaped. He ran
with the hare and chased with the hounds.

I'm enjoying the stout and the others' talk
but he badgers me,
'We'll have a big night out, the two of us,
we'll travel far and find a pair
and none will know, there'll be nobody

the wiser.' And I say 'Aye'
and turn the talk to the ass's age,
her use for foddering, and mention
rain and local news — a death, a sale,
a harvest saved — but he has me in a cage

and starts up again,
'Are you married yourself, *a mhic*?'
'I was never asked.'
'Sure you've maybe no need, you've maybe
a woman who'll do the trick.'

'You know how it is . . . '
I give nothing away, driftwood
on the tide of his surmise
my answer. But I need the ass
and only say 'Be good to that good

woman of yours' though I think to myself
'May your young possess her quality'.
We settle a plan to collect the cart.
He's drunk and I'm linked by one request,
teasing his yes, fending our complicity.

The Conny Ward

By name and nature Conny Ward.

His father knew the faction fights
and saw evictions in the Famine
and he stole land in de Valera's time.
He moved the marks in dark of night.

These men from cottages and cabins,
of poaching and *poitín*,
they are the true heroes:
their sovereign thought was Ireland.

They toiled and thrifted and had
much ado, took travelling trades
and hurried home, and Tom Ward bested
each of them, their friends and faraways.

They fought the Black and Tans
and wintered in damp ditches.
Without their kind there'd not be
a Republic. They saw the sheep and cattle

maimed. 'That was the worst,
to hear the innocents in pain.'
And saw less meals than mealtimes.
Now they remember well and wish

they could forget, unlettered men
who studied tales while harrowing
and told to file away the nights.
When Conny spoke you'd stand

in snow to listen, so still
you'd hear grass grow. He'd tell all
from the root to bloom, hatfuls of things
to mind today and all tomorrows,

and now he's in the hospital
and made wear silly spectacles.
He's 94. The spiders of age
have woven grey webs in his hair.

The eyes that spotted Granard Spire
know visitors by voices.
Still 'you're a great man, Tom'.
'I was. I was.'

Brothers

I hadn't heard a word he said
because he spoke so quietly
and because, the night it was,
we were quiet as nuns in a library.

Four in the morning —
had someone woken and not stirred
from bed we might have passed as cattle
grinding stones along the bank. A word,

a glance could put an end to shadows
in moonlight and lamplight
on water, flickering here, there,
moving upriver. As if by second sight

John Joe went first, walked down the ditch,
and worked his way back along the riverbed,
testing the ground. He said little
or nothing, nothing we heard. A spearhead

glistened — he might have been Neptune,
Brittanica on English coins,
or the devil himself, in one hand a trident,
in the other a torch, as he purloins

the world's lost, lazy souls,
but we had salmon and trout
in mind, and John Joe seldom missed. Fish kicked
and bumped along the headland, in the boot

of the car, and tumbled from the scales
as we drank cups of tea
and fumbled with rough cuts of bread.
We talked of nothing else. I'd give them willingly

away but someone's sure to thank you in a pub
standing next or near
a bailiff. We were votaries of darkness.
By this nightwork I witnessed grown men adhere

to their own laws,
crying out *I want to live my life*.
We made a plan and each of them began
his own return to the world and his wife,

to the light of day. There's a way in which
we'll always call each other 'Brother'.
I'm at it still, I'm still in the dark
putting one foot in front of the other.

The AGM

His suit doesn't fit,
his tie's too tight.
He knows the sun and the stars
shine in other places
but he doesn't feel right

at the Pedigree Sales,
the Charollais Association dinner,
or the Texel Society AGM.
He'd sooner be tangling over stock
where there's hardly a sinner

in shot of an ear or in sight,
or at the turn of a lane
for the setting of meadows. That field's
in great heart; they were always
kind acres — his undisturbed train

of thought. Remember the way he'd let on
to be buying a beast and then sell two?
As if home were a place
and not a time, in a car in the carpark
after the mart, he'd tell you

himself, That's better,
now I know where I am —
where his tongue belongs to the small talk,
the giving out, the praises, say,
of that Charley heifer or that Textile ram.

Winter Work

Friends are unhappy; their long night
finds no day, their lane no turn. They wait
for things to change, as if history
happens to others, elsewhere. They hibernate

in dreams and fear. And Cathryn writes from Dublin:
she lies awake at night and hears
the noise of cars on Rathgar Road,
far from where her life coheres.

I warm to winter work, its rituals
and routines, and find — indoors
and out — a deal of pleasure, alone
or going out to work with neighbours,

a *meitheal* still. All I approve persists,
is here, at home. I think it exquisite
to stand in the yard, my feet on the ground,
in cowshit and horseshit and sheepshit.

The Heartland

Some come to stay and see the farm
and know my friends and say
I'm lucky, but though I love my life
I know it's just one way,

good, and right for me, not better
than another necessarily. I lie in bed,
enclosed behind a mile of wall,
and think about a Minnesota co-ed

who opened to me on a famous strand
about the ghosts of Vietnam,
the telegram that changed a mid-west
farmer's family. She must think I am

the man her brother cannot be.
She is nineteen, near demented.
She rails I'm out of touch.
She thinks I'm too contented.

The Irish Times reports the Kerry babies'
inquisition, another senseless slaughter near
the border.
I know men and women as much in fear

of day as night.
An hour's drive from Orange halls, apocrypha
of fife and drums,
the hole-in-the-wall of South Armagh –

we never had to wait and wonder
if outside worlds might queer
this pastoral. Last night young Farrelly
fished a lake not ten townlands from here

and found the body of a baby girl
dumped in a blue pillowcase.
It's likely that a local mother
is learning there's no hiding-place.

My plaintiff struggles to decide
whether her brother died for nought,
or peace, or the freedom of democracies.
The waste of him haunts every thought.

She wants to notify the world.
She'll join the ranks of press men
in Washington, DC.
Meanwhile she writes to Congressmen.

It's true I chose another course, talk
in small communities, a hope to sway
by carry-on people I understand
and love. I came on a place and had to stay

that I might find my feet, repair
the mark of human hand, and repossess
a corner of my country. I write to her:
our lives are rafts; risk happiness.

If Luck Were Corn

They have found a baby in a lake
not far from here. Slowly the pieces fit.

Her parents slept in the next room
and a girl gave birth. Nine months
their daughter grew and carried
on her own. They didn't know.
They were in the dark.

What happened her
was always meant to happen
to another, somewhere else,
reported in small type,
whispered for a while.

If luck were corn
you'd thresh hers with a whip.
The baby died.

She thought she'd hide the swaddling clothes,
lay the body in the lough,
and carry on. Who'd know?
There wouldn't be a word about it.
No one would be a bit the wiser.

Flesh of her flesh, bone of her bone –
her brother found the body.
Fishing. He didn't know. He told the guards.
The rest you know yourselves. The rest
was in the papers. An inquest. Enquiries.
The question of charges.

That was one week's talk
on Herbstreet's step,
the usual sympathy:
and she only a child herself,
and wasn't that a cross to bear;
and the common savagery:
boys will be boys . . . and girls will be mothers,
she has cried the laugh she had last year.

Until a neighbour stopped their say.
He said, you're great, just great.
You'd carry water in a riddle
or walk the length of Sheelin,
but if you drained the ponds
in your back yards
you'd find more than you bargained for.
You'd not let on,
but the like of that's gone on to yours
since the year of One.

Seven Letters Beginning With . . .

'Essence of morphia, compound of cocaine —
If I could only sleep again . . . '
He has drunk himself into the ground
where a want survives, under the weather.
His days on dry land are a hurricane.

Now he's back on an ocean liner
you'd think he might escape —
he has nowhere to go. His library,
his records mean little now.
He has run aground on the cape

of himself.

꩜

You might have heard his fortune
on the news at one o'clock — famous
for the first time in his life,
a body out of his brothers' shadow,
broadcast for being anonymous.

In a small hotel in Harcourt Street
with a false name on the register
and travelling light, unsteady feet
on the threadbare pile of the bottom stair,
when the porter greeted, 'Goodnight Mister,'

'It's *Doctor*,' he declared.

꩜

'*I* was the physician who couldn't heal
himself.' Oh he'd solve a crossword.
He'd finished *Finnegans Wake*. He'd cure
the captain, crew and passengers. Doctor at sea,
a captain in the army — the fine lines blurred.

'I have no will — I have a wish
my anchor slips
without any pain for anyone and I drift
into a quiet cove where the natives
aren't inquisitive about a ship's

doctor on ship's leave.'

∽

'Season of mists and mellow fruitfulness . . . '
he savours beneath his breath as he stands
at the window in another man's suit
and empties his pockets. Small change.
He must summons himself from the hinterlands

to cover his tracks. No clues.
No traces. The punctilious programme
proceeds — a scalpel excising every tag
and label, a hypodermic needle
unstitching every stitch of a monogram.

He pares away his fingerprints.

∽

Eye to eye with the begetter,
far beyond fear or the thought
of sin, he tightens the tourniquet
and flicks the tip of the syringe.
Essence of morphia . . . Counting to nought

he flexes the muscles of his right thigh.
Compound of cocaine . . . He is humming
the closing bars of a concerto.
He'd be strung on a blackthorn tree
in the *Inferno*. Slowly he's becoming

no one in particular.

D-day. Deadline.
'Oh if only he'd talked
to me, if he hadn't
without as much as a by-your-leave
or a backward look just walked

away, my lost son . . . ' His secret son.
He might never have known the panic
of a man ravenous for a glimmer
of recognition from anyone
whose blind response turned his ways *Titanic*,

his mind *Marie Celeste*.

Easy now. So long waited for,
the desperate remedy
so carefully rehearsed the clock
begins to stop. He's relaxing
like a river eye to eye with the open sea.

Nothing stirs. Wind or wave.
Halcyon days at last, his poise
preserved in the slow wash of the undercurrent
which conducts him to an island
where the trees are fruit and the boys

are friends.

My Care

Sometimes we sit in Phil's
and watch a film, *Hill Street Blues*,
or something. But this is new –
we make a point of turning to the news.

A kidnap, check-points, searches,
killers on the run.
The peace-keeping force can't keep
the peace. The new law is the outlaw gun.

The government debates. Here and there
it seems the talk goes on forever.
Talk, talk, talk . . . After a while
it could be a chimney fire, or bad weather.

Should I do more? Is it enough
to keep a weather eye and talk to friends?
I honestly don't know. All I ever wanted was
to make a safe house in the midlands.

'How's all your care?' I'm asked.
'Grand. And yours?' I don't repeat
my worry for my care, my country. When I go home
the animals are healthy, safe. There's that.

I go inside and stir the fire.
Soon I'm sitting by a riot
of kindling, the soft explosions of seasoned logs.
They have shaken the roots of that familiar quiet.

Holidays

The night is a sick child.
Fits and starts.
Sheets wringing wet. We eavesdrop
on a troubled dream.
We have come to distant parts

to stay with friends
and wake at last
to the latest news from the North.
A body was found in West Belfast . . .
The usual backdrop as we break fast.

Far from the land,
we are chewing the cud
of tiredness. He was shot
in the head . . . bound and gagged . . .
His family objects to the method

of murder. They have lost sight
of the cause.
Down in the harbour
cormorants hang out their wings to dry.
They crashland to their own applause.

Our holiday home's windswept
between a hard rock and a boulder.
We're all at sea. The stars
that should be on Frank's hill
are over my left shoulder.

The Woman of the House

It's not that I minded at first.
God knows the warm word
was welcome.
Such thoughts — and me my age.
Soft talk and silly sayings slurred

into rough touch.
He'd push and forage
and him back from the town
and not within an ass's roar of himself.
Was this his notion of a marriage?

Was this why I stayed home?
As long as I draw breath
I'll ask myself
is this the cross I earned?
Sometimes I'd wish I was for death.

And none to tell a thing
except himself, my own brother.
We'd been so close
we'd eaten off one plate.
It got so bad the other

night I had to go out
to the shed.
Again. Then the world was draughts
and shadows, a thread of light
beneath the kitchen door, an unsaid

worry. I waited there
an age until his ravings ended.
Then he began to snore
and I stole home to say my prayers.
The peace of sleep ascended.

One Day

There will be milk from the cow
forever; no prices
to pay for a harvest
in every season. No hex. No spell.
There will be no need for sacrifices.

Now they tell about a well
near here, a hermitage,
where a cripple hauled in on a litter
wandered home on his own steam,
when their whisper broke the pledge

of silence with the story of the woman
with the one and only child.
'Time you were in second gear.'
'Time you went back to the well.'
They didn't know her thought that blood defiled

the prayer of every month. And no,
there wasn't any stir, no touch
that brushed and quickened. They didn't think.
And someone said, 'You mean to say
he hobbled in with a crutch

and sauntered out without . . . '
I do, and it's true.
'Then what happened to the crutch?'
Someone threw it on the ground.
And one day it grew.

Big

Big as a barndoor. Big
and awkward.
Like a bullock at the bar
at the trough of his own stall,
always and only the bad word

talking to none.
Hard as nails, but soft
in the head. All sulks
and slobbers, and dog rough.
He'd eat hay off a dirty loft.

They were drawing him out,
getting great mileage
out of a row somebody raised
around and about the mess he made
of the second cut of the silage,

the usual boys. And one
was saying, 'You know the way
he'd maybe lend you a hand
at the hay — well he'd charge you
a week and a half for the day'

and that after leaning
since noon on the fork
grumbling for tea and mumbling aloud,
'If I'd left with the others
I'd now be the *Taoiseach* of New York.'

Then he turned on your man
from where he slumped
and grabbed him from behind,
held him in a bear hug,
and humped. Humped.

Silence. Then they started putting chat on him
about all he'd suffered for the Cause,
the blows for Ireland, burning haybarns
and big houses. Wasn't he great?
Oh he was. He was.

He'd count pennies
on the counter of the shop
and peg pounds across the bar,
a small one for himself,
a smoke. He wouldn't stop

to eat except a sister gave him
dinner. You're great, she'd say, just great,
you'd free the nation late at night
but couldn't clear a downpipe in the light
of day. He ate the pattern off her plate.

Himself

Long before the father died
there was something the matter
with your man,
but that's when he took to the fields.
He slept the latter

dozen years sheltered
near sheughs, in winter sheds.
He'd hoosh the heifers
from their lying
and settle down in their grass beds.

A woman left him dinner
in a dish.
Sometimes he'd take it,
more he wouldn't.
They'd a wish

that he'd come home
but not a hope.
He was wed to the four winds.
You might as well be rowing
with a rope

as ask. He kept within
a hen's race
of the place, seldom seen
but sometimes heard,
the base

sound that he made
all laugh
and no laughter.
His beard a bush,
he was chaff

of the whole world's threshing.
Wodwo. Sweeney. Troll,
who did no wrong.
They took him handcuffed
to the hospital

and clipped his nails.
He stirs early
still, a child of fields and gripes,
the intimacy of open air,
and whispers near an orderly

about himself as someone else:
He's not the sort who dares
the devil in his den.
He wouldn't try to teach
the priest his prayers

but they, they know
it all, that crowd.
Let them sing loudly
when they've harrowed
all he's ploughed.

History Questions

They say I wintered and look well
and I reply, 'Can't help it'.
I know they think I've failed.
I'm not the man I used to be.
I'm all spray and no spit.

They are humouring me, an old man,
who have come to ask me history questions.
Because my father met Parnell.
Because he welcomed Pádraig Pearse.
Because there were suggestions

it was he first named The Oldcastle Review
what Arthur Griffith asked to use, *Sinn Féin*,
in a letter afterwards. Because my family fought
on both sides in the war of brothers,
and that after their long campaign

together. Not that it got them very far,
the fight to hold our land and homesteads.
They quickened Irish life a while –
look at us now, *Sinn Féin 's ár gCairde*,
we're still at loggerheads.

Oh I knew famous and good men,
Lance Sheridan, The Conny Ward,
and Benny Hetherton, though books seldom record
their likes. But I'd great time for them
before they went to their reward.

And if it was our uncrowned king
who held my father's hand, what about it?
He was a decent man by all accounts
and he was wronged,
though some still doubt it.

Whoever coined that phrase saw it
demeaned. They're no great shakes,
the men that bear it now,
though once they were. Whoever
learned a thing from history or mistakes?

It's now I care for and about.
When I think back it's 1933 or 4
that comes to mind. For it was then I think,
I think I'm sure, the woodcutter's daughter
showed me honey on the forest floor.

The River

He is whipping the air into shape;
the flies he has tied
drift dry as a bone.
He has taken an element
in his stride.

He is driving them on,
the waterway horses,
flailing the crop of upcountry spawns.
Beneath is the grain. Splashes
are chaff of whitewater courses.

He has stepped into the same stream
often and recently seen it putrefy.
He has loved a place
he'll feel a need to leave.
They had to milk the good cow dry.

He was making light but not little of
the tarnished hallmark
of the bank, the copper line,
dank overgrowth. He was making
light of midsummer dark

when we were fishing and thinking
with a friend. 'There's a lake,'
wrote a man, 'deep
in the mind of everyone,'
and he was making a mistake.

It's a river.

An Open Fire

He hears the cowherd calling home the cows
and says out loud, Can it be so late?
The boss cow turns her head and flicks
her tail. She has come to an open gate

and she goes in. He is making his way toward
a circle of warmth and welcome, an open fire.
A man full of years. The cows of his life
have herded now to yield in the warm byre.

A Way of the World

A lost light shines
in the haggard
of years. So much begins,
like a pearl, upon a blemish.
Some take life hard,

some take the same life
easy. I'd sooner sing
heartbreak nor cry it.
But a baby's born, the baby
dies. Who knows anything?

A Fortune

She whispers 'Stay'.
You lie by her side.
You touch the silk
bandages.
            Resist the will
to caress her breast.
It will fill
into a fortune of milk
for the baby who died
on Saturday.

A Part of Ourselves

in memory of John Fallon
born 7 December, died 8 December 1990

Forewarned but not forearmed —
no, not for this.
A word first whispered months ago
and longed for longer tripped on the tongue,
a stammer, now a broken promise.

Averted eyes. Uncertain talk
of a certain strange condition.
The scanned screen slips out of focus,
a lunar scene, granite shapes, shifting.
We bent beneath the weight of attrition

knowing it might have been worse.

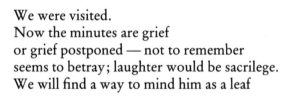

We were visited.
Now the minutes are grief
or grief postponed — not to remember
seems to betray; laughter would be sacrilege.
We will find a way to mind him as a leaf

who fell already from the family tree,
crushed. He hadn't a chance.
We pray at best for the open wound
to grow a scar.
We welcome him his deliverance.

There are things worse than death.

Imagine a man not wanting to live
who could. Now he lies in an oxygen tent
in the whispered kindness of nurses.
Night and day are one to him,
his without hunger, just bewilderment

and quiet uncomplaining. Brightly lit.
He seems to breathe another air.
There's a photograph in *The Best of* LIFE:
A summary execution, Budapest, October 1956.
He flinched that way from the snapshot glare

of the world laid out for him.

So they gave her sedatives.
I sought and found the comfort of a friend.
She tendered brave communion
in the early hours
as I waited, waited, for the given end.

There are more hurts than cures.
Already we'd begun talking
the hushed courtesies of loss.
Then, at dawn, the telephone.
It seems I've been sleepwalking

since.

We broached the sorrow hoard
of women, tales unmentioned in their marriages,
unsaid to friends, to families.
Fellow feeling loosed their tongues
about unwanted pregnancies, abortions, miscarriages,

as his remains, a fingerful of hair,
a photograph, his cold kiss called, 'Remember me,'
and I stood with them at the lip
of graves. She cried from miles away,
'I miss my baby,' as an amputee

laments a phantom limb.

☙

Time and again, for years on years,
I've thought about a corner of Loughcrew,
a three-foot plot for 'Henry Timson,
born and died September 2nd, 1899',
sheltered under ivy-overgrown yew,

and wondered how you'd walk away from burying
a child. Little I knew. Now the sound
of a cousin's prayers and Pa Grimes' spade
wheels me round and her sudden, 'We are leaving
a part of ourselves in that ground.'

The innocent part.

☙

He'll die again at Christmas every year.
We felt the need grow all night
to give him a name, to assert him
as a member of our care, to say he was
alive. Oh, he lived all right,

he lived a lifetime. Now certain sounds,
sights, and smells are the shibboleth
of a season. In a hospital corridor
I held him in my arms. I held him tight.
His mother and I, we held our breath —

and he held his.

A Human Harvest

Our wishes quicken into flesh
and yield a human harvest.
Remembered, revived —
the parts of a family
flock home to nest.

His sister, our daughter —
we clutch her as a text
of faith. He needs to know,
Will she still be here in the morning?
Yes, love, tomorrow, and the next.

PART TWO

The Deerfield Series:
Strength of Heart

for Frank Henry

Who can tell what sorrows pierced our soul.
— John Williams

Beaver Ridge

1

Again the sun rises on Pocumtuck Mountain Range
as it has done so often,
so many times. Again the sun begins
on Beaver Ridge to soften

the edges of the mist
and pry night's lid from the chill
valley underneath. It glances on the rock
and searches out the still

water as it meanders
at the edge of meadows
near a street . . .

2

It was not to be happened on.
It was to be discovered
on a plain where the human
heart's potential hovered.

3

Here was the promise of plenty.
Here was plenty.
Here, after the plants and animals
colonized the continent, the cognoscenti

settled.
Here they sang their reports
of a fertile valley
where a giant beaver disports

itself: Pocumtuck Range.
Here on the esculent roots —
'pestered' with profusion —
on berries, nuts, and fruits,

on bear, moose, and deer,
beneath a sun obscured by geese,
they throve in their agreement
with the place.

Shad and salmon fare at falls,
alewife at the oxbow
of still water. They hunted
and gathered. Then, with fire, axe, plough,

and hoe they tickled the soil.
Three sisters laughed:
corns, beans, and squash.
With equal craft

they tended the seed of future promise.

4

On the children of the woods
and treaties
peace smiled, peace and prosperity,
while in the shadows of the race
a cup began to fill
with treachery.

They spent the earth
as if it were
an endless currency.
They moved their villages
when they looked up
and saw the woods too far away.

They shed the beaver's blood.
And in return received
the gift of government,
of plagues and poxes.

5

Could there ever be a time again
when the past's unsighed for
and the future's sure?
Could there be an end to weeping?

Morning, and the sun begins to shine.
The beaver of Pocumtuck stirs.
In the lodge of perpetuity
it is but sleeping.

Stillwater

The river has reason
to rest
after its rush
down that ridge
before it carries on.

The Buttonball

1560   It took root in a clearing
before white settlers walked
the shadow of Beaver Ridge,
when wild beasts stalked

'and wilder man'. Say a song
for those who, on their last journey,
passed it by,
lost branches of the village tree —

> The wheelwright, the smith,
> the peltry trader;
> the miller, the cartwright,
> the ropemaker;
> the hatter, the housewright,
> the currier;
> the fletcher, the ostler,
> the cross-cut sawyer . . .

Again and again it greened
as they grew up and once grew grey.
Already its shadow lorded over them,
the sir of sky, on Charter Day.

Backfire

1637   Consider how certain things conspired.
As when the English fired
first and someone fired back.

How the natives learned that tactic
introduced at Mystic
and countered with a night attack.

Bloody Brook

Eastwards the Pale.
Westwards scowls
a thicket, crouched
hinterlands, abode of owls

the whole way to the Hudson.
September light transmutes
leaf and vine, and they
who count among the fruits

and profits of the place
fresh water and wild grapes
dally a while
as a train of grain carts scrapes

behind, the 'flower of Essex county',
Captain Lathrop's choice brigade,
at ease until enticed
into an ambuscade

of Indians who, as if
in broken English, mistook,
and blushed, and changed
the name of the Muddy Brook.

Two Miles

Even the mighty Connecticut River
conspires to conserve the rhythm of the place.
It backs up after big rainstorms
two miles to stop the Deerfield race.

29 February 1704

1

A rumble on the rooves
the canter of snow's hooves.
The winds exhaled a moan . . .

Nightwatch away, asleep.
A shadow shapes within
the walls of the stockade
the footprint of a moccasin.

Curt daylight grew
on house- and house-lot burnings,
on women made widows,
on the sounds of mournings.

The sun that stretched from Beaver Ridge
squinted on the solemn
rites to repair sleeping innocence
and helpless age, on requiem.

As bad as slaughter,
as bad as torture —
a body stripped of all
including skin — was capture.

The pitying pines expressed a groan.
No say behooves
all dawn made known.

2

Three hundred miles
on frozen lakes and rivers,
by foot, sleighs,
and elm canoes;
frost grew in suppurating wounds,
heart weak in the bewildered ways.

And later by the power of prayer
one conspired to calm
the boisterous waves
and so bestow safe crossing
on followers
in the name of 'He Who Saves'.

3

How they must have hunched awake
at night in the cold of campfires,
afflicted presences homesick
at the Feast of Dreams and Desires;

how they must have ached
for that other world to live in.
And later still she, who 'married
a savage and grew into one',

looked up, an offspring and a parent both,
that child of many prayers,
looked up and out without a word
beyond her tender years,

and overheard her own father's
proposals and petitions in the oblique
manner of the mediator, their translator.
For his was now a language she could no longer speak.

Mehuman Hinsdale

1709   Consider the case of the man
whose people came to settle and stay,
whose shares broke ground
in 1669
four years before he became
the first white baby born
in the shade of Beaver Ridge,
whose father, uncles, and grandfathers
were killed that noon at Bloody Brook,
whose own new son was slaughtered
in the Leap Year massacre,
who with his wife was captured
and held two years in Canada
before his first redemption.

Consider him on an April morning,
1709,
driving north from Northampton
a team of horses
and a cart of apple-trees;
how he was carried off again,
west through the woods
and overland again to Kahnawake,
to Quebec, and overseas to France and England,
until after more than forty months
he came home, home here,
the horses older,
those apples planted in the ground
and new fruit on their branches.

Piecework

1804–
1864 Consider the case of Lydia Bascom
in fire- and candlelight who appliquéd
and quilted turkey tracks for her trousseau . . .
Are they the stains of rust or dust or sun's fade

on spotted lime and plain camellia?
Or something else? She patterned in a harried
place peace in pieces. They can't have anything to do with the news she never married.

The Street

1962 Something over-
whelms
the street:
elms.

The Stone Grove

Someone carved a pair of posts
as if they were wood,
curved mill-stones, cider presses,
milk coolers, and a well-head.

When they flooded the quarry store
to make the reservoir
at Quabbin they buried ground
in water and said *au revoir*

to the world they'd seen,
each eyed and shafted quern
set in the hubbed sun space
of a zen cairn

on the Upper Level. A rock presides
above the stone collection
which comes to rest quietly. The river
dawdles, and flows on.

The Burying Ground

The voices of stone makers continue to resound.
Listen now. Before it was first woken
down, down in the burying ground

quiet became silence, was dumbfound.
Ages' sorrow and heart's strength betoken
the tones of other voices which resound.

Like ice on a spoor by the memorial mound
the topsoil's harder healed nor broken
anywhere in a burying ground.

For centuries the elders were renowned
for knowing the saved lives' token
was their name passed on to resound

after their entry, run aground,
in the pined, birched, and oaken
grove on Albany Road: the burying ground.

Born to be hanged you'll never be drowned.
Our names are called in the outspoken
voices of hosts as they resound
down, down in the burying ground.

Birches

Shadows cross
the road;
a row of birches:
barcode.

A Shiver

And everywhere
the miracle of trees —

mulberry, oaks,
and elderberries,
sweet-, sour-
and choke-cherries;

poplars, pines,
Cedar of Lebanon,
Norway spruce,
rhododendron;

holly, hickories,
hornbeams, hemlocks,
sassafras, chestnuts,
basswood and box;

catalpa, laurel,
pear and juniper,
cypress, sycamore,
elms, and fir;

aspens, beeches,
walnuts, willows,
magnolia, dogwood,
hazels, and sloes;

birches, birches,
and crab-apples,
silver-, swamp-
and sugar-maples;

birches and maples,
maples and birches,
and all the other lovely trees
shiver in a human breeze.

Bicentennial

A cut stone on a farmhouse
on a corner of Main Street
struggles to convince:

TWO HUNDRED YEARS AGO
NOTHING HAPPENED HERE.
It has been happening ever since.

The Upper Level

January's sunset glow
against the backdrop
of the Beaver's Back
is red brick, pink snow.

Strength of Heart

Who knows what sorrows pierced our souls.
The human heart admits a choice
by way of suffering and grief. Rejoice
in the prudence of a place as it extolls

the election of a spirit to grow
instead of wilt. What were they waiting for
that winter of the massacre, of want and war?
Deliverance? What came? The past is also

ours in all its ways: the quiet boy in his heyday
cut down by his own hand, the public mystery
of the smiling boy soaring over Lockerbie,
and a later boy swept away

from all of us one evening on the Lower Level . . .
Time weaves loose threads into a pattern.
The ghosts of Charter Day, they are not taciturn;
they resonate and revel

in their legacy, a promise which unfurled
like the flag of liberty. That promise kept.
It said there are uncarved commandments to accept.
Be worthy of this life. And, Love the world.

PART THREE

The Heart's Home

Our Lives Now

What will they make of it all
in the ages ahead —
the tractor remains and machinery parts
by Conaty's dismantling shed,
their shreds and shards;
the tyre-hill beside Frank's silage spread;
the smudged note of a kindness
the girl in the bookshop said?

Will we be evaluated
by what we have discarded?
The day we rummaged on Pine Hill
for a fossil or an arrowhead
we took as much delight
in wind music through the head of a fiddlehead
fern. We mind the apparition
of an osprey and egret instead,

where we live now, in a future past.
We don't regret. We treasure all that's bred
to pass away, like fingerprints
on water. The worn thread
was woven honestly and served its while.
The hearth was warm once in the broken stead . . .
And he is still with us, the bundle of the boy
who, in the order of things, will not be dead.

The Bandon Road: Sight of It

You cross a torrent
and the road swings right,
and suddenly you catch sight
of it, where the light
between the woods' improvident

shadow and shade contracts;
and it's beautiful, a rich
stretch of pasture, pitched against the pitch
blackness of the ditch
while, on every blade of grass, it re-enacts

Spring. Because we often blunder
through the world we stum-
ble on our proper lives. I'd just come
back to you and in that delirium
dawned on this array of wonder.

You could search for it all day and night
or adventitiously receive it with the shiver
you'll mark forever, that sliver
of good life lighting across the river,
over the bridge, where the road swings right.

An Easter Prayer

The first forsythia;
daffodils;
gorse or whins or furze
on hills,

in hedges.
Late winter aconite;
dandelions; primroses
challenging the light

of Easter morning.
The lesser celandine;
a yellow fertilizer
bag define

Spring in our steps.
I love my children
and my wife.
Rise all again and again.

Again

Two a.m. and three below
as you go out again
to check a lazy ewe
in labour. Along the road
gale forces bend and burst
the sails of ivy in the masts of ash.
Morning is a gapped tooth
in the smile of April.

The tide of night's gone out
and grounded in cropped grass
starfish that were thistles once.
Sunrise suppressed the mist
around a padded nest. She's cleaned
herself; she's suckling twins.
The herd of gorse is grazing still
halfway up the hilly hill.

A Half-hundred

He was all head and no stout.
A bad egg, and no mistake.
A dead loss.
He couldn't stir his stirabout.

He'd be blowing at the ember
of a deed done long ago.
He'd get up when it was time for bed.
He'd start shearing in September.

He'd pull in outside the Co-op to pass
away an hour the minute you'd a half-
hundred on your shoulder. Live horse,
he'd say, and you'll get grass.

When the sergeant called about the ragwort
he'd the feet up on a sunny day.
Would it do next week or maybe, for certain,
the next one after? Devil the harm or hurt

it's doing a soul . . . When the clutch was just about
to go he'd manage to lend a loan of the car,
or a shovel when the shaft was cracked.
He'd start a fight but not fall out.

If he owed you money, you'd hear, It ill-behooves
the likes of me to carry such as cash.
He'd drive around the rim of your hat.
The borrowed horse, he'd say, needs hard hooves.

St Oliver's

They are cycling from school
   and have come to the cross —
are they the picture of happiness
   or the preview of loss?

They have consummated, these four girls,
   a hundred ways to hesitate.
When it's time to go, 'or I'll be skinned,'
   one of them cries out, 'Wait,

'Wait,' and they pedal away
   in different directions, into parallel lives.
Still something of their talk
   filtered through the hedge survives

for they have tapped the vital topics
   in this everyday interim:
What he said to her,
   and what she said to him.

And I wonder what will happen to them
   when they come to graduate?
Will they separate and each become
   a candidate

for the emigrant's dilemma —
   Stay or go —
and gamble the next referendum —
   say Yes or No?

Two years ago the two of us
   smuggled ourselves across the border
to affirm a prayer that there was neither
   defect nor disorder

this time with the baby;
   the longest journey
we'll ever undergo. We found
   succour in a troubled city . . .

I think of our children, those girls at the cross,
   and entreat a just inheritance:
information, kindness, a chance,
   and then a second chance;

I dream an innocent end to the commonness
   of double talk and single think,
reprisals, revenge,
   the nod and the wink

of parish pump politics —
   jobs for the boys, Euro junkets.
Where they'll soon park in the desperate dark
   used condoms litter St Oliver Plunkett's.

                            (*1994*)

The Cloud Factory

As we drive past the mines
Adam says to me:
They're working hard
in the cloud factory.

Own

A collie pup skims
the pebble of its bark
across the back yard.
It clatters on the slates

of the grainstore by the gate
and instigates its growling
at the echoes of its own
trespass of the dark.

Was the world ever as it seems?
Alice sees and needs no proof.
The heifers on a hidden hill
are standing on a hayshed roof.

Gate

There's no track of a hedge,
no trace of a fence.
In the middle of a field
an iron gate and no evidence

of path or passage.
It clings to rusty hinges
on chiselled stone,
it hardly infringes

on the course of stock —
for cattle a pair
of scratching posts,
for the colt and chestnut mare

a nuzzling place where you pause
and again you contemplate
in the middle of open grazing
your fate

by a gate that stops nothing
and points nowhere . . .
Say for a moment
the field is your

life and you come
to a gate at the centre
of it. What then?
Then you pause. And open it. And enter.

New Country

He was singing that old country song:

    'I was drowning my sorrows,
    They were learning to swim;
    I was thinking of her,
    She was thinking of (him) . . .'

when he started to think,
Who said the cure for love
is marriage? Or, waiting ends
if you wait enough?

And when one of them said,
sometime after the incident,
'I'm sorry. I love you . . . '
And one of them didn't.

Northern Lights

Sunset on our hill
an hour ago.
Now I watch it
from a window

five miles high.
Five miles below
the lights of settlements
suggest a congruous tableau.

The wing-tip pulses
like a glow-
worm in its rhapsody.
I don't know

where we're going.
I marvel at the way snow
smoothes the wrinkles
of the days and know

you possess that power too.
Morning will show
us where we are.
Meanwhile we're incognito.

Whoosh

Now, then, and again.
Here and there.
Like an apparent
whoosh of air

the ghosts of winter
embody the frail
bounties of pines
as they unveil

by falling. Woods
and woodland paths inherit
their wafer rush.
What did you do to merit

that soft stampede,
you wonder, as it falls
again and startles you,
as if someone calls

to you from faraway,
some sprite apostrophe.
You turn around. You see.
You see there's no one there to see.

Meeting in Maine

for Karen and John O'Brien

1

Mud and muck of stamp and roll.
Slurp and slobber showed
they'd met their salt needs
by the margins of a back road

in Maine. I'd wanted years to see
this throwback that the wild refined
and suddenly came on a place they'd been.
So we met in the mind.

On a broken branch the actual,
a shock of their molt hair,
gave me to understand
it's enough to know that they're out there.

2

A believer. I could have followed,
scat to scat, or fitted
my footprints to their bruting
of the beaten path,
signs of great-witted

hoof and contradicting
dew claw.
But I stood and looked around
and wondered if from woodshade
one was watching me, in equal awe.

3

Bog rush, pond weed and water lily.
Dogwood and willow, birch and balsam.
Alder, aspen, mountain ash —
leaf, twig, shoot and stem —

constitute browse and salvage
by the burns and beaver meadows
where they calve in quiet places
after the rut and meet in brawly wallows.

4

I'd wanted room for everything,
for creatures in the wild,
I was thinking as I headed home
to my family and friends,
reconciled

to never seeing those great ungulates,
and restored, a footloose
pilgrim in the northwoods,
to whom appeared suddenly a cow
and then another, a bull, and then a pair, moose

everywhere, and then more moose.

Harvest in Spring

As if the roof itself
were crucified
and wept its charity
through stigmata;

as if the trees themselves
thawed into a scatter
of buckets as they released
high notes which dripped

and lowered as each vessel filled
along the edges of a wood
or stubble field
or by the margins of the houselots

in the hill towns;
as if an orchard spilled
itself when the avalanche of Autumn
was stored in barns of memory

and the year appeared in sap
carted from the taps to sugarshacks.
Beneath the snowless rooves
pine smoke and steam

conferred a harvest out of season,
in March and April's
nectar, sweet yield
of swamp- and sugar-maples.

Happy. Loving Women

Four. Swinging on a five-bar gate,
my mother watching; well.
Evenings on a pony, riding the range
of anywhere, under a spell.

Then I became that solitary
boy with a ball
to catch and kick against
the goalposts of a gable wall.

From Osnabrück to Lennoxbrook
I grew up in the care of loving women.
Loughcrew. A maple in late May
blazes Japan.

Work and, after work, the ease.
Now I overhear
the children's play — and them
still friends. Music to the ear.

And once, just recently, I brushed
against her breast and felt it harden.
The woman of the fields
has strayed into the garden.

World Peace

Cherries like ours
on their cherry tree.

Rock islands
in a gravel sea.

Ryōan-ji Temple, Kyoto

The Heart's Home

Celebrate a place for them,
the wildflowers:
forget-me-not, wood sorrel,
pimpernel, bloom of laurel.
Commemorate bog asphodel
by the wooden gate to the bluebell
wood. Treasure easy hours.

Let there be room for volunteers,
root growth of shrubs and trees.
Let bramble breed, with honeysuckle,
crab apple, and witch hazel.
Let Old Man's Beard and fuchsia
cry their hearts out on montbretia,
cow parsley, and wild strawberries.

Let there be animals
and other wildlife there.
Let teasel charm gold finches
beside bracken, where ivy inches
along branches and a drystone edifice.
Let it be a healing place,
where the heart releases care.

Long live the weeds
and, yes, long live the wilderness.
A clump of thistledown flies
down beside a pair of butterflies.
Peace settles
there, among couch and docks and nettles,
convolvulus, and bittercress.

Let's reunite there, love,
where refuge clings like mistletoe,
where the heart's home, where you bestow
your open invitation yet or
grant your kiss. Your kiss lingers like a love letter.
Marry me again before you go.

Storm at Sea

Winds ruffle the grey hairs of the waves.
They go against the grain
of fields shut off for silage.
Gulls plant themselves inland
in the grazing. They flourish

when a tractor passes
or an edgy collie grumbles.
They say kissing's out of season
when the flower's gone from the gorse.
Though this'd shear the leaves off ivy

the headland's sanctified by petals.
Can this be happening to happy people?
I think of all I should have told you
as I dream into a summer fire.
And my eyes are hands: they hold you.

Notes and Acknowledgements

Two of the poems in Part One appeared in *The Speaking Stones* (1978), seven in *Winter Work* (1983, 1986), eighteen in *The News and Weather* (1987), and fourteen in *Eye to Eye* (1992). The first three of the above collections are out of print and will not be reprinted. Part IV of '*from* Eye to Eye' hasn't previously been printed. 'A Human Harvest' was published first by Wake Forest University Press (NC) in *News of the World: Selected Poems* (1993), a book comprising most of the poems from Part One in this collection. My thanks to Dillon Johnston.

page 38 *beestings:* first milk, colostrum, containing antibodies
page 51 *meitheal:* a co-operative workforce

Grateful acknowledgement is also due to the editors and publishers of the following, in which some of the poems in Part Two and Part Three were published first: *Agenda* (London), *Albany Road* (Massachusetts), *Asheville Poetry Review* (NC), *The Café Review* (ME), *College English*, *Éire-Ireland*, *Janus* (NJ), *Metre* (Dublin/Prague), *Poetry* (Chicago), *Poetry Ireland Review*, and *The Recorder* (NY).
    The Deerfield Series: Strength of Heart was published in a limited edition, with woodcuts by Timothy Engelland, by The Deerfield Press on 1 March 1997. This poem was written in response to an invitation to commemorate the Bicentennial of Deerfield Academy, 1797-1997.

Deerfield, in Western Massachusetts, was the frontier outpost of the English settlement of New England. Beyond it was beyond the pale. It was the site of celebrated historical events — among them, in 1675, in South Deerfield, the 'Bloody Brook' massacre and, on the Leap Day of 1704, a savage attack by the French and allied Indians and a march of captives two hundred miles to Canada. Inevitably, it was the location, too, of many smaller tragedies. Now the village, in the fertile Pocumtuck Valley, accommodates a number of farms, Historic Deerfield, and Deerfield Academy, one of the country's superior private schools. I have tried in the poem's various parts to enter history, geography and mythology to comprehend a place and its fate. I wondered, How do we live in a place? Sometimes by suffering, certainly.

The poem is an 'occasional' one. But what does that mean, and when is the occasion? Now? The original Charter Day? Or might it include 'occasion' as in a 'happening' or 'event'? In the final section, I tried to imagine the utterance of a commandment, which is an invitation, too, for the original aspiration and the ongoing accomplishment of the Academy. It demands that communities, and families, try to be, as Hemingway wrote of a character, 'strong in the broken places'.

I thank the Trustees, the Headmaster and faculty for creating the conditions for my stay in the course of a 'sabbatical' or retreat from The Gallery Press.

The title *News of the World* was prompted by one of the late John Jordan's encouraging reviews of my early poems. Dennis O'Driscoll's support for the idea of this book was crucial. The friendship and example of Seamus Heaney and Paul Muldoon have been vital and sustaining.